Lovers
Are Future
Enemies

Ron Gavalik

Pittsburgh Poet

Copyright © 2019 by Ron Gavalik
First Edition

Published by Pittsburgh Poet
Pittsburgh, Pennsylvania
Author: Ron Gavalik
Proofreading and Editing: Rebecca Hoffman
Cover Illustration: Pittsburgh Poet Contributors

ISBN-13: 978-1-7320697-6-3

Experience more works by Ron Gavalik at
PittsburghPoet.com

For the sluts,
the beautiful dames
who've made the best lovers
and incredible friends.

I once met a vampire named Evelyn.

You read that right, a vampire, a beautiful night creature who embodied the suffering of the damned. The exact year eludes me, but it was a Monday night in an empty pub in Pittsburgh, just after the last of the winter snow melted in the late 1990s. Sitting alone at the end of the bar, she drank whiskey sours. Much like me, the young woman appeared to be in her mid-twenties. Long brunette hair veiled part of her face and she wore some kind of concert t-shirt under a black leather jacket. The way she held that whiskey glass and subtly dabbed at her mascara tears with a napkin revealed to me an old soul who'd grown familiar with struggle. As she gazed out the window, her dark eyes contained sorrow, regret, a dull ache of the soul. There is no English word that defines this state of mind, but the Koreans call it *haan*, a term derived from so many generations born into oppression.

I finished writing a few lines about the lack of human empathy in society, and then closed the notebook. It has never been my way to engage strangers in bars. Drunkards believe themselves experts on the world. The women will treat you like shit until you prove yourself worthy. I usually can't handle those games. This dame's peculiar spirit, however, drew my attention, and so I moved to the stool next to her.

'Hey. I'm Ron. How's your life?'

'Evelyn,' she said, without looking at me. 'My life? You don't want to know about my life.'

'Sounds mysterious.'

The beautiful stranger drained her glass. She then called the bartender over, a wrinkle-faced guy in a worn plaid shirt who looked ready for retirement. He didn't talk much. We both ordered refills.

'Mysterious is a word to describe a cool cat,' she said. 'I can assure you, that's not me.'

'Me either. I just scrape by.'

'When you're like me,' she said, 'life is death and death is life. There's nothing to live for or die for. You just trudge on because it's all you know.'

'That's a cheery message. You must be popular.'

Evelyn half chuckled in a sad kind of way.

'You look pretty upset. Anything I can do?'

'Absolutely not.' She squinted at me like I was crazy. 'I don't know you, dude. Besides, the only thing anyone can do for me is too much to ask.'

The bartender slid another whiskey sour in front of Evelyn and another bourbon on ice in front of me. He walked over to the TV at the other end of the bar to flip through the channels. We were the only people in the joint, and he clearly didn't give a damn about us.

Evelyn gripped the plastic stirrer between her thumb and index finger and stirred in a careful rhythm. 'The cheap sours mix these bars use can separate from the bourbon,' she said. 'Back in the old days most bars used lemon juice with sugar. One of the hotels I frequented in the late 1960s added egg white to the mix. That gave it some froth.'

'The sixties? You weren't even born yet.'

Evelyn sipped her drink and then went back to stirring. 'I was around.'

'How is that possible?'

That dame looked straight at me and slightly opened her mouth. Right in front of my eyes, two fangs descended from her top row of teeth.

'You get it now?'

'Holy shit,' I whispered. 'You're a...'

'Yep. Don't worry about it. I won't hurt you.'

'But...'

'Get over it, dude.'

I drained my whiskey. Evelyn's lips, her face, her body, they appeared normal, if not stunning. She'd shifted her focus back to the window. Her hair shimmered as satin under the dim lighting. The logical part of my mind couldn't accept such a fantasy. Still, I'd witnessed something I couldn't explain. As a young writer in search of truth, art had become the study of people, the constructed landscape of our lives. Deep in my bones, I believed her myth.

'I have so many questions.'

'Too bad,' Evelyn said. 'I'm not in the mood.'

Her matter-of-fact attitude threw me off. 'Damn, lady. You sure are surly.'

'I'm fucking hungry. What do you expect?'

'I'm assuming you don't mean a burger.'

'Correct. I haven't had a drop in weeks.'

'How come?'

She looked down at her glass and exhaled in frustration. She again fiddled with the drink stirrer. 'It's so hard anymore.'

'You mean the killing?'

Evelyn ignored the question. Perhaps she didn't have the patience to discuss her problems. We sat silent for a few minutes. The bartender had finally landed on a sitcom with a laugh track. I couldn't help but think about how our lives are filled with propaganda, persuasion, the big con. We can't even be trusted to laugh or weep by our own natures.

'For about 35 years, I thought I became numb to it,' Evelyn said. 'You do something immoral enough times and the mind becomes accustomed to the behavior. Your brain shuts down. The psychological consequences diminish.'

'Yeah,' I said. 'I know exactly what you mean.'

'But I think I was repressing. About a year ago, something

inside me cracked. I was going down on this yuppie in his car
out in Robinson Township. I had him all relaxed, you know.
His guard dropped. All I had to do was tap in.'

'What happened?'

'I just couldn't do it. It was like the muscles in my jaw
locked in place. My conscience stopped me.' She paused and
looked up at the ceiling, her lips pursed to fight the regret
that oozed from her pores. She quickly pulled it together and
refocused. 'Let me tell you, that shit is tough. I mean, it's an
addiction, you know? It's a fucking drug, not nourishment
like they say in the movies. The withdrawal is ugly.'

'So, you just deny yourself?'

'I force myself to go through with it every so often. I mean,
I have to. But I wait until the hunger drives me mad.'

'What would happen if you refused forever?'

'I really don't know. I'm afraid if I wait too long, I'll go on a
killing spree or some shit.'

'Has anyone ever offered you a little, you know, but
without sacrificing their life?'

Evelyn snorted out a chuckle. 'You mean like draft beer?'

I shrugged at the analogy. 'Sure, a pint here and there,
kinda like donating at a clinic.'

'Are you kidding me? No one would go along with that.
Everyone who learns my truth goes out of their way to avoid
me. Some of them I've tapped. Others have moved away.
Most of the men I meet, they just want to fuck me.' She
snorted again. 'Tapping those assholes is far easier.'

Watching a woman deal with internal torment has never
sat well with me. As a child, my mother regularly fell into
torturous bouts of crippling depression that I couldn't fix.
This time was different.

I finished off my whiskey and then rolled up a sleeve.
Evelyn watched as I stretched my bare arm out in front of

her. 'Here you go.'

The dame pulled some hair away from her face. She looked at my arm and then into my eyes. 'No way. It's too risky.'

With my free hand I grabbed the brass rail that ran along the front of the bar. 'Go ahead. Hurry up.'

'No. That's too much. If you're trying to get me in bed, all you have to do is pay the tab.'

When you know the world doesn't give a shit if you live or die, there's a sense of self-worth in helping others. 'Look,' I said, 'this is a spontaneous moment you're killing. Either get to it or I'm leaving.'

Evelyn's eyes glossed over. She could have easily killed me and moved on. For a brief moment, however, that vampire held the appearance of an exhausted, vulnerable young woman who could no longer lift her emotional shield.

'Uh, okay,' she said. 'If you're sure.'

'Yeah, it's alright.'

Evelyn leaned over the bar. Her hair sensually caressed the underside of my forearm. She then wrapped her lips around me to form a kind of vacuum seal that tugged at my skin. Inside a split second, the vampire's teeth moved through my flesh like butter. My body went wobbly. I clung to the brass rail for balance, but also to suppress the instinct to pull away.

'Remember,' I said, 'just a pint.'

The bartender took his eyes off the TV and glanced over at us, a perturbed frown pulled across his face. To this day, I believe he was a little jealous.

After fifteen seconds passed, Evelyn picked up her head, inhaled deeply, and then licked her lips. She grabbed a couple of napkins and pressed them over the bite marks.

'You'll clot in a minute. Hold these firm.'

I tucked my arms under the bar. 'You get what you need?'

'Holy shit, yes. That'll keep me good for a month.' She scanned me up and down, her eyes almost smiling. 'I don't understand how you could do that. I had to really fight to stop myself from draining your ass.'

Rationally thinking, she was right. I didn't know the woman. Only a madman trusts a stranger with his life, let alone a murderous vampire. Still, there was something true about her spirit. I've always had an increased emotional intelligence, an ability to judge character. I took it on faith that she valued the gift; therefore, I believed she'd keep me safe.

'Listen, there are people with ambition,' I said. 'They have money and power. They're meant for big, awful things.'

'Is that you?'

'Fuck no. Some of us fly under the radar. We pour the cement and cook the meals and write the words for others.'

The gratitude in Evelyn's eyes drooped. She formed a slight frown. 'I have to fly under the radar, too.'

I reached across the bar, napkin stuck to my forearm and grasped her hand. For the rest of the evening, we sat quietly together drinking, thinking, breathing a little easier. Out on the sidewalk, we said our goodbyes and then went our separate ways. No phone numbers were exchanged, no long friendship or romance forged. We helped each other. That was enough. A beautiful woman needed someone to give a damn. I needed a reminder that my life is worthy of others. I have no idea if Evelyn still exists. If so, it's nice to think she remembers me and our sympathetic evening.

I will never forget her.

Acknowledgements

When I set out to compile a collection of free verse poetry from my observations and so-called romantic experiences, I'd hoped to publish a sarcastic and humorous body of work. While some of the truths contained herein may bring a smile, I've found that many of the pieces continue in my tradition, to expose the dark underbelly of our lives. My truth is my truth, and I refuse to change the raw meaning of my words for the sake of marketing, otherwise known as the continuous con. I'll let you be the judge of my absolutes among the storms of relativism.

Writing the poems in this autobiographical collection happened over 20 years of lonely, maddening nights. Some of these thoughts began as journal entries. A few are web-based conversations from online dating websites. Most are my experiences from long-term relationships, short escapes, and brief encounters with women around Pittsburgh. The words are snapshots, moments that represent our entire lifespans.

Lovers Are Future Enemies would not exist if not for the patronage of the two most supportive TRUE Readers an author could ask for: **Holly Kudyba** and **Rebecca Shortman**. The absolute power of spirit that lives within each of these respective mothers, daughters, friends, and impassioned fighters is unmatched by anyone else I've ever had the pleasure to meet in my travels. I won't reveal any personal secrets here, but I can assure you, these two women navigate the fires of struggle with grace while so many others crumble from the darker forces of the world around us. Rebecca and Holly are the leading contributors of a small band of devoted TRUE Readers who generously support my literary pursuits. Those amazing souls are the reason I record my truths.

No acknowledgements can be written without including my most trusted literary ally and editor, Rebecca Hoffman. Rebecca's devotion to modern publishing and to my work means everything to me. Any success I achieve is largely due to the confidence I have from Rebecca's red pen and her constant companionship on our journey.

I must also thank the authors, bloggers, journalists, and other opinion-makers who celebrate my work. Without those psychopaths, my words would never reach the public. I am grateful to that community, of which I am a humble member.

The romantic relationships we forge are simultaneously important and absurd. Sometimes I wonder if there are angels in heaven that look down upon us and scratch their heads in confusion. Every one of us has felt love for another. Some of us have allowed that love to morph into control or a form of violence. Others have allowed the heart to rule their lives and have fallen victim to its constant follies.

When we look back on our romantic lives, it's hard not to laugh. After all, is it not the purpose of life to forge memories from our sweat and tears? We archive some of our moments with film, words, and sentimental artifacts. The most potent of life's histories, however, are kept in vaults behind the fire in our eyes. Occasionally, we unlock the tumblers and privately revel in those experiences again.

I've decided to crack open my vault for the world. Just as I exposed many transgressions in Slag River Sins, I'm now pulling the curtain back on some of the bizarre and intimate moments I've shared with members of the opposite sex. Some of this material might be considered offensive. That hardly matters. Truth does not take a holiday, nor does any battered soul that insists on chasing the sun wild and free.

Now, pour yourself a drink, something that bites the back of the throat. Find a comfortable chair and allow these words to flow as a river's current over your eyes, your lips, your mind. We're going for a ride to explore that which makes us excellent lovers and tragic characters. By the end, it's my hope that you and I will be bonded until they lower us into the grave.

—Ron Gavalik

"Men are absolutely crazy. I mean, they're really nuts. The women are worse, but that's not my problem."
—Old woman on the bus

1

We loved, laughed, and fucked
so hard, death was impossible.
The Grim Reaper recoiled
his bony hand in fear
of our wild spirits.
When the love faded,
I taunted the Reaper.
I dared him
to come for me.

Real Supposition

'I don't trust men,'
she said in that surly voice
that I once found seductive,
but now drove me to rage.
'Always trust people to be people,'
I said. 'The human experience
is designed for survival.
If you hand us your heart,
we will cradle it
for a while.
But baby, when the hunger comes,
most of us will feed.'

Succumb to Pleasure

The more you resist,
the more I know
your legs will spread.
Over the years, I've learned
your battle is not with me,
but with the temptations
of dark internal pleasures.

The intoxicating malice
that awaits us
is spliced with pain
and the ever forbidding
sensation of sin.

Blank Canvas

She and I sat on the sofa
together.
She didn't speak,
her face a blank canvas.
I stared at the rounded folds
of the curtains
in thick silence.

The sadness that night
was something went wrong
and I just didn't have
the desire
to figure it out
or fix it.

Simple Thought

Sat comfortable in my chair,
I penned verse about truth
and violence and love.
A few feet away, she stared
out the window,
her eyes conveyed a pain
I didn't have the tools
to relieve.
Sometimes it's simple
to be the whiskey poet,
yet so fucking difficult
to be a man.

Single Issue Lover

That unique way
she bit her bottom lip
when the sadness came
made me fall in love.
I often made her sad
to keep the love going.
Eventually, the day came
when she left me
for a new man
who fell in love
with the way
she smiled.

Dating Site Interaction #214

Her: My daughter left me.

Me: I'm sorry. How come?

Her: She said I'm drinking too much.

Me: Is that right?

Her: I told her I don't get drunk. It's called dating.

Me: That's the best definition I've ever heard.

Her: What do you mean?

Me: Hemingway said it made other people interesting.

Her: Huh?

Me: Hilarious.

Musical Inspiration

That young dame,
she sat up straight on the sofa,
her legs closed, her mouth shut tight.
'You drink too much.'
I didn't respond.
'You should go to a gym.
Lose some weight.'

I closed my notebook,
drained the whiskey,
and then climbed out of the chair.
'Let's go for a walk.'
I opened the back door.
She stepped outside.
I then locked the door
behind her tired ass.

While pouring another drink,
the dame banged on the door.
'This isn't funny. Let me in.'

The thumps and screams
became a form of drum music
to which the typer and I
went to work on some verse
about beautifully failed lovers.
The music stopped
before I'd finished
that poem.

Marrying Type

A short, heavyset woman
strolled into the South Side coffee shop.
She oozed sexuality through her plaid skirt
which resembled a Catholic school uniform.
It draped over her generous hips
and that young, round ass.
A Slayer t-shirt stretched
around her huge breasts.

The poem I'd been writing that day
was lost, obliterated by desire,
as I watched that creature
of seduction and pleasure
order a coffee to go.

As my metal chick made for the door,
with coffee in hand she paused,
and took notice of my staring.
'Like what you see?' she said
in a tone that bordered the fine line
of sincerity and sarcasm.
I nodded, my mouth partly agape.
Any words my mind formed
were displaced by a raw hunger
to watch that woman grasp the toilet seat
in the bathroom and to hear her moan
while I fucked her deep from behind.

'Oh, goodie,' the dame said
and then she shot me the finger.
'Now, go fuck yourself.'

My words still wouldn't come.
All I could do was gaze
as the object of my passion
swayed her hips out of the joint.

For a moment, I considered chasing
after the woman and marrying her,
but once she was out of sight,
that moment quickly passed.

Drunk Heaven

At this sushi joint,
a date searched for the words
to describe her raw fish dinner.
'It's heaven,' she said,
'it's definitely heaven.'

Call me a simpleton, but in my view,
divinity on Earth is kicking back
the night before you swindle a sick day,
the sweet tinge of bourbon,
the smoke of an acid 60 gauge
that rolls over the tongue,
and some Pink Floyd
with the lights off.

Temp Match

All she wanted
was more sleep.
All I wanted
was more drink.
The match felt good
for a short while,
but even Heaven
must collapse
at some point.

Strikes of Love

Every time you kicked me
in the balls
or clawed my face,
I could feel your love
and your sorrow
within the energy
of each blow.
Now that you're gone
and that sadness has ended,
there's an apathetic void
in the back of my mind.
The absence of your rage
reminds me
it is better to have bled
and healed
than to have never
suffered at all.

Devoured

You don't hate me
because I fucked you.
That's far too simple, baby.
I communed with you,
and I devoured your spirit.
From the husk that remains,
you must find wisdom
to regrow that which you were,
and know life will never be
quite the same.

Milk and Dignity

An old girlfriend and I
walked upon the sidewalk
to the grocery store.
The cement felt right
on that fall day, after
a humid summer.

'You walk too slow,' she said.
'I don't walk, baby, I stroll.'
'Well, it's frustrating.
I like to get there,
not piss around.'

We continued in silence
for a moment
and then I said,
'It's all about the pace.
At your pace, life flies by
as a confusing blur.
At my pace, I see things,
the bugs fighting to survive,
the cats styling their fur.
I gaze into the eyes
of passersby. Some of them
are present, taking it all in.
Others have lost their minds
to the wolves, the slavers,
the politicians.'

The girlfriend didn't respond.

Instead, her pace slowed.
She held my hand, and rested
her head on my shoulder.
We strolled together
on a quest to buy milk
and to reclaim the years
we have yet to live.

You're Still With Me

My love for you has remained,
even when the phone calls stopped,
and my cock ran dry.
Thoughts of that one day,
the memories visit
during mundane moments.
I'm just letting you know,
in case you're curious.

Reprogrammed

You never had a chance,
did you, baby?
The beautiful soul that flickered
with fury behind your brown eyes
is now gone, strangled
by villains who thirst for power.
You're now part of a group,
a demographic, an agenda.
The person you were is gone,
but I remember.
I will always remember.

Dating Site Interaction #628

Me: Hello! I see you're into the outdoors. Favorite activity?

Her: Great

Me: What's great?

Her: Your saying

Me: Good thing I donate to the Literacy Council.

Her: Great

Wings and Regiments

On a dating site, I asked Nicole
to meet for a drink and an appetizer
at a chain restaurant-slash-bar.
The woman had good legs and full lips,
but she hated her job as a secretary
for a construction company
that operated out of some rat hole.

We sat at the bar. After a couple drinks
Nicole and I laughed about politics
and she let me massage her thigh.
Things felt alright between us.
'How about we drive into the city?'
I said. 'We could sit by the river
until the sun comes up.'

Nicole tilted her head to the side,
reluctantly tempted by the idea.
'I have work in the morning.'
'Fuck it. Call off.'
'What? No. They need me.'
'You're one of those loyal girls.'
'Isn't that what men want?'
'Some men, sure.'

We ate our chicken wings
in silence. My thoughts wandered
as I considered a world
where the bosses and customers
could let two people sit together
by the water and laugh.

Music Together

She asked why
I chased her so hard
after telling me
about her sins.
That girl didn't understand.
She was my scratched
vinyl jazz record
and I was her
flea market
turntable.

Silent Rage

On the sidewalk, in the spring rain,
that woman scowled at me hard,
the way a lion eyes its prey.
She stood motionless, silent, soaked.
The rain, or tears, rolled down her cheeks
and dripped from her chin.
An invisible rage radiated from her aura
that struck instant fear in the current of passersby
who rushed around her on that gray day.

My soul had been murdered before,
and so I figured, why not again.
Under the awning of that coffeehouse,
all I could do was not give a damn.
I lit my acid cigar and puffed
until the smoke clouded my vision.
That day, I would die or I would live.
Either way, there was no sense trying
to control events or time,
when the inevitable rebirth was certain
and would change everything.

The reasons for the standoff
and its conclusion are unimportant,
mere details we've all lived
and forgotten.

Sever the Grip

Bethany lived alone
inside a quaint apartment
in a wealthy suburb.
She always went to bed early
to maintain her complexion.
Before sex, Bethany locked
the bedroom door behind us.
After several nights, she told me
the door severed the world's grip
from around her soul.
I chuckled at Bethany that night,
but a few weeks later, I locked
my bedroom door and slept
in the deepest peace.

29.5 Days

I only loved you
for a day,
but that day
went on
for a lunar cycle.
When we departed,
I knew we would never
love anyone
quite the same.
When the expectations
are low,
the rewards
are served
in greater portions.
The sweet aftertaste
lingers.

Irritating Scars

The days she went mad,
her eyes danced in their sockets
the way a lion paces inside its cage.
Her fingernails, man,
they dug through flesh
like a psychotic who jams
a broken beer bottle into your arm.
Those jagged shards
of her soul are still embedded
under my skin.
They're the sharp regrets
of an unfulfilled life.

Pedal Hard

Standing next to my bike
on the sidewalk of a city intersection,
I waited for the signal to cross.
A bus opened its doors
and out stepped this woman,
the truest dame of grit I'd ever seen.

When our eyes met, the world faded.
In that brief moment, we fell in love,
got married, and bought a home.
As the years progressed,
my health failed. Life became labor.
The day I finally went, my love sat
in the chair next to the bed,
the place where she read
all those indie novels about struggle,
and she held my hand.
'Have a wonderful journey,'
she said with that smile
that taught me redemption.
I then closed my eyes for good.

Back on the sidewalk,
that love of my life was gone,
so I jumped on the bike
and pedaled hard
toward Point State Park.
I needed to see the fountain
set against an orange sky
as the sun dropped
behind the river.

Voyage to Happiness

'What the fuck is this shit?'
Alyssa said, waving her smartphone in my face.
I could see she pulled up an old poem
I'd made public over social media.
'It says you liked fucking someone else,
but that you don't love her, and you bailed.'
An inartful characterization of the work,
but truth, nevertheless.

Every time I cross the threshold of dating
to the investment stage with a woman,
I make them promise to not confuse
the interpretation of my written life
with the relationship in front of us.
It's a promise women always make
and never keep.

'Relax, baby. It's not about you,'
Alyssa crossed her legs on the sofa
and she tucked her hair behind her ears.
This time she meant business.
I drained my whiskey and ginger ale.
By the end of the conversation,
I'd submit to her demands
or be shamed for living.

'I know it's not about me.
That's not the point,' she said.
'How do I know you love me
when I read this kind of stuff?
Maybe you're using me the

way you used her.'

'I don't use people, baby?'
Don't assume fucking is a commodity
or a transaction. You're not an ATM.
You're better than that.'

Alyssa pulled a blanket over herself
and wept into the cloth.
I moved to the sofa,
massaged her shoulders,
and gently kissed her neck
until the sobbing stopped.
That night, she rode me harder
than usual. Her pussy felt tighter.
I wondered if jealousy can grant men a ticket
for a voyage to happiness.
Maybe, but I figured
most of us lack the courage
to survive the journey.

Adventures

Thick memories of driving
to pick you up
and carry you away
for mini adventures,
they visit me often.
I rescued you from solitude,
and you rescued me from myself.
Sometimes when I drive alone
to the jobs or the grocery store,
I pretend we're chasing the sun
in pursuit of those lost days.

Unravel

I once dreamed
about your voluptuous lips
that formed these addictive smiles.
They gave me peace and hope.
Now I'm haunted
by your malice, the pleasure
for the destruction of life,
in those cold eyes.

While I regret allowing you near
that loose string
you pulled to unravel my life,
I'm relieved to still have
the small part of my spirit
you did not consume.

Dating Site Interaction #569

Me: I really love whiskey.

Her: Do you know how to love a woman?

Me: I love Fridays too.

Her: What the fuck?

Me: You know what I really love?

Her: Apparently not humans.

Me: I love a courageous spirit.

Her: Do you think I have courage?

Me: Much like confidence, if you have to ask...

Her: Sometimes I'm courageous.

Me: Sometimes is all one can expect.

Her: I'm horny.

Me: Yeah. That's pretty typical this time of night.

Her: You want to fuck or what?

Me: Sure.

Stroking

Her kink was to watch
as I stroked one out in the car
in suburban parking lots.
One night, a guy in a ball cap
walked by. That poor man
was her unwitting accomplice
to ecstasy, but he just shook his head
as he strolled into the pharmacy.
I figured stroking was easier
at home on my own,
but that's the shit
we do to see
them smile.

Reject the Instructions

I tried to love you
the way you needed
and mount you
in the customary manner.
It just didn't work
for me,
and it will never work
for you.

I hope someday you find
your own truth.
When that day comes,
I know you will finally release
all of that passion and zeal
to reject the instructions
of parents, friends, lovers, others.
I sometimes imagine how glorious
that moment will be.

In the future, I will see you
strolling on the sidewalk.
You will look different, self-assured.
Your stride will carry a grace
that shows the world
my wish was fulfilled.

The Good Fight

The dame from the North Side
with the missing fingertip,
she had a beautiful edge
as if she shaved her tattooed thighs
with a straight razor and bar soap.
Sex oozed from every pore.
Under a full moon, she admitted
romance gave her spirit power.
In that truth, it was easy
to smell the desperation.
Later I learned
that woman simply hungered
for the tools to go all the way
in the good fight of life.

Memory Erased

I don't remember
that time we fucked in the woods
and laughed at the squirrel
that insisted on watching.

I have no memory
of that summer afternoon
when you wore black leggings
and we walked across the city.

I've completely forgotten
the taste of your lips
after late night drinks.

There's nothing that can be done
and no one who can force me
to remember.

Agenda

Lily's hands were soft.
Her red nail polish
didn't contain even one chip.
As that dame stroked
the inside of my thigh,
the scent of an agenda
lingered on her breath.
So I started the car.
We didn't speak five words
the entire ride back.

The amazing taste of buttered toast

One dame needed to be raped
in the mornings for energy
to start the day.
'Smack my ass,' she'd say.
'Pull my fucking hair.'
I performed as instructed,
but all I ever really wanted
was coffee and a moment's peace.

The evenings were better.
She'd suck my cock to get me there
and then climb on top.
She rocked her hips
in a slow, hypnotic rhythm
for a few minutes until I came.
We would then sleep a few hours
and begin the cycle again.

After getting home one day,
I found her crying on the sofa.
'We're on different wavelengths,'
she said. 'We aren't the same.
We want different things.'
I didn't bother to argue.

When she left the house
for good, I breathed relief.
The next morning, I brewed
a large cup of coffee
and ate buttered toast
while gazing out the window.

Free of the morning violence,
I watched a rabbit hop in the grass.
It stopped and moved its ears.

To this day, I'm not sure
if it was the rabbit or the solitude
that made me smile.

No More Love

I loved you
until I didn't.
That's how it goes.
I'm sure the answers
are out there to be plucked
like cherries or heart strings,
but I have none of them.
Leaves fall. Hearts break.
Whiskey is swallowed.
That's life.

Scorched

I've grown so tired
of hating you,
but I've hated you so long,
it's all I know.
After the foul odor of death fades,
fresh air will replace
that which we cannot change.
Staring out the window,
my chest tightens from dread.
The pollution we've spewed
may have scorched the soil
where new trees must grow.

Dating Site Interaction #797

Her: I think I'm a pretty awful person.

Me: Send nudes.

Her: Guess I'm not that awful.

Me: Precisely.

Her: Wait, do you really want nudes or are you trying to show me how awful I'm not?

Me: Both.

Her: Ugh...

Me: Life, baby. It is what it is.

Hardened Hope

The woman with the tattoos
across her chest and the troubled past,
she needed to be controlled,
dominated in what she called
the most invested form of love.

Young men of sex and violence,
they refused to understand her qualities.
The dummies called her slut while
users called her far too infrequently.

Over so many years of bad choices,
the tears that once washed her clean
no longer flowed. Hardened
by the emotional vacuum,
that woman who walks with style,
she now consumes novels and music
to escape the struggle.

Still, there is a flicker of hope
that can sometimes be seen in her eyes.
Thoughts about the good times
bring about the occasional smile.

Silent Split

I knew it was over
the moment I breathed
a deep sigh of relief
after you slammed the back door
and drove away
to have coffee
with a friend.

Easy Stroll

We held hands
on our walk to the breakfast joint.
The sun slowly warmed the air.
An elderly woman at the bus stop
smiled at us and said,
"I love Sunday mornings."
Church bells in the distance
and a flock of birds taking off
brought her words to life.

Walk Away

There was a time
when the sight of your lips
made me want to rape you
inside bar bathrooms
and atop the kitchen counter.
Those days are now gone,
and I no longer have any desire
to own you. There is nothing
remaining inside to give or say.
So I will walk away
alone, upon tired sidewalks,
to never love again.

You Are My Truth

I remember loving you
a long time ago,
before I appreciated
the songs of spring birds
or the city skyline at night.
I just didn't know you yet.
Now that you're mine,
after a lifetime of struggle,
doors close right the first time,
less whiskey spills onto the counter,
the universe makes sense.
Thank you for that gift.
You are my truth,
now
and forever.

2

Fools in bars and coffee shops,
they insist on talking to me
about life and love.
They don't get much of either.
I tell them, 'No one will love you
until you love yourself.'
That's when they wave a hand
in my face and loudly disagree
with that truth.

First Death

There was this woman,
short and curvy,
with big tits and red curly hair.
Everyone said 'don't date her,
she's a crazy bitch, a man-eater,
her eyes can make a man kill.'
I took the warnings to heart,
but life those days was to slog
through wading pools of shit.
Besides, the spiraled descent
into Hell's gaping mouth
is more enjoyable
when someone is there
to push you in.

Decadent Temptation

Cookie crumbs left behind,
spread across a coffee table,
they are the physical remnants
that represent the cold morning
after a drooling night of passion.

Sometimes we cannot resist
a sweet and decadent temptation.
After we've consumed enough pleasure
to satisfy the desire of sin,
the residual twinges of guilt,
the emptiness,
and shame
are unavoidable.

Those crumbs splayed in front of us
have the power to wreck our sanity.
In a selfish need for preservation,
we then turn our backs
and walk away.

Aftertaste

A terrible lover is similar
to a terrible piece of chicken.
You can choke it down
as expected or cast away
the remnants
and move on.
Neither option is ideal,
but only one
is grounded in truth.

Blood Sport

Dating is a blood sport
where one must scrape for life.
If the match is won,
you help each other limp
together as champions
through the struggles of time.
If the game is lost,
you stare out windows
alone, always wondering
about the life
that could have been
had you triumphed.

Trust me on this one

Always love the woman
with bruises and scrapes
on her legs,
the remnants of sorrow.
She's the stallion
whose heart runs strong
with a wild felicity
for life.

Dating Site Interaction #163

Her: I think u might be a good one

Me: Thanks. I got them all fooled.

Her: why u so liberal

Me: Everyone deserves a home.

Her: they need to earn a home!!!!!

Me: Who is 'they,' and earn it from whom?

Her: the job

Me: Do you have a home?

Her: I live in my besties

Me: Exactly.

Her: ur not smart huh

Me: Nope.

Angel Whores Lost

Where are the whores,
the imperfect angels
whose lips once oozed desire?
Women of struggle, baby,
they swayed their hips and stomachs
with confidence upon sidewalks.
The angel whores apologized to no one
as they inspired wretched men
to march on and struggle and bleed
as honored warriors
for the slightest taste
of their salty flesh.

Vanquished by false prophets,
the once-confident angel whores
have been replaced
with self-loathing and doubt.
On quiet whiskey nights, their absence
is mourned. All that remains
are potent memories that
run naked and wild and forever
without restraint.

Daily Realities

Inside the café, a cute artist
with blackened fingertips
sketched in her notebook.
A handsome boy took the next table
and waited patiently for a chat.
Sketching with a fervor,
oblivious to her surroundings,
that artist and I shared a truth.
Imagination is often preferable
to the daily realities
thrust upon us.

Confront the Demons

In line at the movies,
a middle-aged woman spoke
to her male companion about life.
'I have the worst time sleeping,'
she said. 'I have to pop a pill.
I'm a pill popper.'

Thumbs hooked in his pockets,
the man tilted his head and smirked.
His business casual tweed jacket
told me he agreed.

The woman then laughed
in a sick, sad kind of way.
Her voice was entwined with grief,
perhaps for a former life,
a failed promise from a younger self
that things would be different.

A desire bubbled up inside of me
to tell the woman to stay awake
and paint, drink, listen to music.
But I kept my mouth shut.
After all, we must slave
for each meal.

The truth, however, doesn't change.
No matter how many miles we run
or how many soot-covered hills
we climb, the quest for escape
in drink or drugs or sex

will not cure the sadness within.
The only cure for grief
is to face our demons
and free ourselves
to grieve.

Hidden Mercies

There's magic in the world,
and although I've not received
much of its unexplained mercy,
I've seen it happen to others.
When the lonely can laugh
from the gut after many tears,
that shit is magic.
Playful cats and slutty women,
healthy shits and vitamin C,
and the relief that comes
when she walks out
and you know it's over,
all of this is pure magic.
We just need to see
these small moments
as the gifts they are.

Reckless Contour

An older woman at the bar
danced alone near the jukebox.
Eyes closed, she swayed her hips
to some kind of old school jazz.
Cigarette smoke hovered around her
on the makeshift dance floor.
The smoke contoured to her body,
it clung to her reckless past.
The chain-smoking drunkards
hollered and giggled as cowards.
One of them would fuck her
before the night ended.
All I could do was watch
and write this poem
in my mind.

Fuck Me Calm

The jobs and the bills,
the tedious and the boring,
they've always worn me down
to the last strokes of a pencil's nub.
Other men fall into pits of madness
when their women run their mouths.
Those guys don't realize,
hysteria is the perfect distraction
that makes the heart pump with passion.
A good fuck calms the nerves.
It also provides temporary relief
from the debtors and their threats
to wring out the last drops of blood
from our stones.

Sunday Truth

I love you.
Yes, that's true.
I don't even know you,
but I know you embody unique
stories of humor and sadness.
There's so much hatred
all around us. That loathing
has taught me a valuable lesson.
I love you. I always have,
and I always will.

It's Enough

The old woman hung around the bookstore café
most days, just to get away.
She wore her coat in the summer
and added a hat in the winter.
Her voice quivered
when she told me her husband is dead.
She now lives with the kids.
They won't let her buy books.
She has too many books
about love and cooking and artists.
The old woman's husband loved books,
but now he's dead,
and the kids,
they say it's enough.
Still, she hangs around
because books are what she knows
and the books are what she loves.

Dating Site interaction #292

Her: Hi

Me: Hi back. Your profile says you're in Salt Lake City.

Her: Yep

Me: Utah?

Her: Yeh,not mormon tho

Me: You know I'm in Pittsburgh, right?

Her: Yeh,ur not mormon.

Me: No, I am not.

Sunday Fist Bump

A beautiful young woman
sitting at a sidewalk table
penned cursive words into her journal
and she smoked a fat cigar.
'Hey, baby,' I said.
'Where'd you get that cigar?
I wanted one,
but the shops are closed today.'

She looked up at me
through her round sunglasses.
'I got it yesterday.
I love to smoke when I write.'
That dame got out of the chair
and stood in front of me.
Her legs whispered erotic stories
of loving sexual moments.
'I'm a wind sign.
How about you?'

Before I could say something rude,
a young man popped out
from the bar behind us.
'I'll be ready to go in five,' he said
and then he was gone.

The dame removed her shades.
'That's my boyfriend.
He's an earth sign, no emotion.'
She looked down at the concrete.
'I like that, though. I just wish

he would keep some comments
to himself. But at least it's healthy
...yeah, we're healthy. I just wish
he wouldn't talk about fucking
old helpless women.'

I raised my fist to chest level.
'Bump it, beautiful.'
She made a fist and brought it
to my knuckles, holding it there
for at least two seconds
while gazing up at me.

I'd learned a long time ago,
the wisdom people seek must be lived,
not q-tipped into a stranger's ears.

'Keep reading and writing
and exploring,' I said.
'Your truth will come.'

Brick Wall

A young woman leans
against the wall
outside of a useless store
in a useless suburban town.
The woman cradles a cigarette
between two fingers.
She stares at the screen of a smartphone
between long, satisfying drags.
This woman pays no mind to the people
that stroll by. They don't matter.
She's above it all, a slave
whose mind transcends
the limits of time and space.
The deep red color of her fingernails
and the black eye shadow tell me
a story about a time in the past
when someone once tried to own her.
Through struggle, she made it
to the other side,
and now,
no one will ever try
to own her again.

Snuffed

She raged.
I absorbed.
Later, she died.
No one understood
how or why.
I knew.
She used anger
to contain deep guilt
until its corrosion
snuffed out
her flame.

No Ass (istance)

On the bicycle trail, a middle-aged
woman in spandex biking gear
had her bike flipped upside down.
I dismounted next to her.
'You need a hand?'

The woman kept her eyes fixed
on her bike wheel. 'Why would I need
your help?' she said, her voice filled
with contempt. 'It's only a flat.'
I didn't respond.

Pedaling along the river,
I made the decision
to keep offering assistance.
Surely, someday I'd need it.

Inventory

At the bar, a guy
with wild curly hair
sat hunched over his beer
'I'm in a loveless marriage,'
he said to anyone within earshot.
'Get a divorce,' the bartender said.
Crazy hair didn't immediately respond.
Instead, he swallowed the words
along with a mouthful of beer.
'The marriage is worth saving,' he said.
I dropped the paperback of Ginsberg.
'Doesn't sound loveless to me, brother,'
The guy smirked. He then raised his glass
as if to toast the ghost of his former self.
The bartender took inventory of his cooler.
I went back to my book.

Chin Up

I've always preferred women
strong enough to not give the finger.
In a world of ugly cowards
and beautiful charlatans,
the dames who stroll by
with good posture,
they really got it
where it counts.

Replacement Emotions

The number of emotions
we temporarily replace with fucking
is absolutely astounding.
The way those emotions
come back at night
with the force of a sledgehammer
to take certain revenge
on our notions of self-worth,
that's also quite amazing.

Crosswalk Grace

Standing on the street corner,
an old man wearing a driving cap
leaned on a metal cane.
He gripped it with determination
the way a soldier grips a weapon.
'You going to club someone
with that thing?' I said.
That old timer kinda smiled.
'Too many women after me.
I have to fight them off.'

He limped through the crosswalk
with a sense of style and grace
most of the men I've met
would never achieve.

If you want to know...

If you want to know
where to find the gambling,
ask a bartender.
If you want to know
where to find Jesus,
ask a prisoner.
If you want to know
where to find love,
ask yourself.

Cleansed and Soiled

There was this one day
in the summer,
we held hands and sat quiet
on top of a picnic table
in a park near a soccer field.
We heard the giggles
of children whose pure spirits
had not yet been murdered
by ambitions or objectives.
Those happy sounds washed over us
as bath water after a hard day.
Then we heard the vile timbre
of the parents' voices whose souls,
poisoned by fear and resentment,
would not be redeemed.
That's when we chose to leave
the park. I have no desire
to ever return.

Fulfillment is Robbery

I waited ten long, hungry years
of adult life to date an exotic dancer.
As a young laborer on construction sites,
not yet old enough to drink,
the older guys always found a way
to sneak me into the strip bars on paydays.
The way those girls moved on stage
and their courage to go nude
inspired both lust and admiration.

Years later, I got together with a woman
who told me she'd once worked as a stripper.
I explained my eagerness,
and she agreed to grant
that wish.

After that beautiful spirit rode me to completion
in the back of the car, she flopped on the seat
next to me and said, 'We solved that problem.'
I sat there in silence, physically satisfied,
yet mentally drained. The fulfillment
of that simple-minded desire
robbed me of the dream.

Entwined

The words flow smooth
onto the typer
when my belly is full,
the bottle has a few hits,
there's a dame ready for me,
and my ass wipes clean
the first time.

That's the life, baby:
food, women, drink, shit.
You might think our lives
are similar or entwined.
They are.

Don't worry.
I'm pretty sure
that's the way
it has always been
and the way it will always be,
especially when we hate
the very idea.

Spellbound

In the liquor store,
a Native American woman strolled by,
browsing the white wines.
She wore a choker made of beads
and long gold earrings.
The woman had to be 55 or 60,
but her body still had the right curves
in all the right places.
Her eyes burned, baby. They had fire
that told stories of a never-ending war,
brutal lovers and laughing children,
victories, defeats, tears,
and, after many years,
straight up survival.

Frozen, I couldn't move.
The whiskey bottle in my hand fell to the floor.
That woman then looked over at me,
we stared into each other's souls.
I needed to have her,
be inside of her deep and long.
I needed to feel her hair on my chest
and consume her breath.
That woman, she had answers
to the questions I never learned
how to ask.

'Do you need help?' she said
in the way a mother asks a child.
The spirits wouldn't allow me to speak.
Instead I just shook my head.

The woman kind of rolled her eyes
and walked away.
I picked up the whiskey
and skulked around the back of the store
until she checked out at the register
and departed from my life.

Stress or Pain

The brunette with the tattoo
on the bottom of her back,
she was the one I wanted.
That woman stared me down cold,
her face twisted in disgust.
The very idea of my penis
made her want to vomit.
I couldn't blame her.

Further down the bar,
a heavyset dame winked at me.
She had three long hairs
that clung to her chin for dear life,
and very thin, very high eyebrows
drawn onto her forehead.

I finished off the whiskey
and then strolled out of the joint.
Some men get the best
women, cars, and jobs.
The rest of us must choose
between stress or pain.
That truth made me chuckle
on the drive home.

Soft Distraction

When life refuses to go
your way, and the madness
takes control, drink looks sexier
than that one dame at the bar.
You know her. She's the distraction
with the red lips and troubled eyes,
the one every drunkard in the joint
wants to press against
to remind himself
his problems are trivial
when compared side-by-side
to her nightmare.

Dating Site Interaction #388

Her: I have more kids than I said on my profile.

Me: Your profile says you don't have kids.

Her: Yeah.

Me: How many children do you have?'

Her: I have five kids.

Me: Really? How old?

Her: They range from 10 to 20, but they're independent.

Me: A 10-year-old is not independent.

Her: True.

Me: What did you expect to happen here?

Her: I want a good man to take care of us.

Me: I don't think that's going to fly with me.

Her: A good man wouldn't care.

Me: I never get tired of hearing that.

Fast Healing Wound

A teenage boy leaned
against the wall at a local mall.
His eyes stared down at the pavement,
shoulders slumped, a smartphone
dangled from his hand.
The late summer breeze
carried the faint scent of cookies,
that elusive form of happiness
we want to believe can be sustained,
but so often slips through our fingers.
Don't worry, my young friend.
More cookies will be baked
tomorrow.

Impolitic

Outside a cigar shop on the sidewalk
a skinny dame in a dirty skirt strolled toward me.
'You like having your dick sucked?'
Her voice carried a tone of indifference.
'You a hooker, baby?'
She tilted one of her green high heels
to the side and crossed her arms.
'Sex worker, not hooker.'

A dump truck drove by.
It released a blast of diesel exhaust
that formed a toxic cloud
of economic stability.
'I used to enjoy blowjobs,' I said,
'but I'm not so sure anymore.'
'You a fag or something?'
'Nah, just exhausted.
Everyone has an agenda.'

The hooker smiled, revealing
several rotted teeth.
'At least I'm honest about it.'
I nodded and then lit up
my acid 60 gauge.
'I'll see ya around,' I said
and then walked west up the sidewalk.
'Fine, faggot.'
The clack of her heels
on the concrete faded
as she strolled
in the opposite direction.

Choice

When a man can hear
a woman's screams and sobs
thunder across an empty parking lot,
from a lone truck
partly hidden by the blanket of night,
that man is faced with a choice.
He can ignore the cries
and continue to move forward,
or he can turn and fight.

Such terrible options are rarely requested,
and no matter which decision he makes
that man will be haunted
during the quiet moments
for the rest of his life.

Consumer Windows

Every so often we'll read an article
about a man who cut his woman's flesh
into little specks of bloody cornflakes.
Sometimes a woman will run a butcher knife
through some drunken husband's scrotum.
Consumers scream these people
have snapped or suddenly went insane.

We usually fail to consider the truth
that madness is rarely on display
in the store windows and screens
that govern most aspects of our daily lives.
Far too often, we project onto others
values and desires streamed into the mind,
rather than study our lovers
for who they really are.

Imposed Morality

I often read social posts
and overhear coffee drinkers
discuss the betrayal of friends.
The stories are always the same.
A man or woman placed an expectation
onto someone else, and that person
failed the imposed moral test.

Maybe it's because I'm older
or that my grandfather raised me,
but I learned long ago
expectations are the tip of the sword.
Trust is about understanding people,
their thoughts and desires,
and how they behave.

Trust your pals to be flawed,
beautiful, ignorant creatures,
who will succumb to temptation.
Armed with this truth,
you can't go wrong.

Rite of Spring

The sidewalks on Easter
are empty for the most part.
Few well-dressed parishioners
walk to and from their churches.
A sexy woman with red lips
wearing a little dress and heels,
she carries a cake. Her stressful frown
indicates she's marching
to the obligatory family dinner.
The sun shines bright.
A light breeze carries the chill
of lost friends.
In the distance, one can almost hear
voices call out in unison,
'He is risen!'

Good and Plenty

I've fallen in love
with every dog
that has approached me
on sidewalks,
about half the cats
in windows,
and 1/3 of the women
in bars and cafés.
That's plenty of love
for any man.

Road to Hell

A man and a woman in their twenties
sit in front of me inside the coffee shop.
The way they talk at each other
and smile at each other
indicates this is their first meeting.
The woman hides behind
a mask of makeup. She strokes
an ATM card with her fingers.
The man hides behind
crossed arms that cover his stomach.
On his wrist, the guy fingers a digital watch
with a plastic band.
Neither of them speak a word
of truth or consequence,
yet they both laugh these empty laughs
of desperation and hope.

I think they will fuck tonight,
get married in a year,
and then wonder when
it all went to Hell.

Treachery Mourned

I've always mourned
the saps in bars who claim
total devotion from their women.
When a dame walks out of the house,
temptations lurk on every sidewalk.
A man cannot expect to keep a lady
when there are thousands
of better men with better jobs,
better religions, and bigger cocks,
who are so much easier to love.
Some guys know this truth.
They work a little harder
to keep what they have.
Others drink in bars
and run their mouths
while their hearts break.

Insecure Freedoms

My first apartment
had two rooms and no windows
above a butcher shop
on Broadway Avenue.
I figured it would hide me
from the bill collectors.
Sometimes I chatted to people
just outside the door
while they waited for the bus.

One time, a woman twice my age
with a jagged scar on her cheek
agreed to come inside and fuck
if I drove her home afterwards.

I really miss that apartment.
It had character and courage,
the insecurities of freedom,
and not a bug in sight.

Red Dream

A young woman stands on the sidewalk
in front of a vape shop.
Her long red hair is the dream
of desperate men
that flutters in the cool spring breeze.

This woman of destiny,
she fiddles with her smartphone,
her thumb quickly scrolls screens
in a futile attempt
to fight boredom.

She's waiting, waiting, waiting
for her next adventure.
Those skintight yoga pants
and her filthy sneakers,
they tell me
she does not have long
to wait.

Proof Through Actions

The brunette in the pub
with the milky long legs
that contained the occasional bruise,
she knew how to find serious action.
Every bloke took his best shot,
even those old drunkards
whose cocks stopped working
before the Millennium
tried and failed.
For all of their wasted effort,
she chose me, the quiet poet
at the end of the bar.
'Do you want me?' she asked
while pulling at my front pants pocket.
'Yeah, baby, I want you.'
'Why do you want me?'
Everyone outside of the madhouse needs validation.
I thought about her playful question.
'Because everyone else wants you.'
She smiled the big smile of a commodity,
revealing three yellow teeth
among the off whites.
She then took me back to her place
so that I could prove to her
and to myself
that romance can exist
between the lines
of our greed-stricken lives.

The Right Way

If you read my words
drunk on whiskey or wine,
and while getting licked
by an unpredictable lover
who owes you money,
you're doing it right.

3

Love is to feel a pain
that ruins lives.
Commitment finishes us off.
One must suffer in style,
die gallantly,
and then make an art
of the rebirth.

On Demand

Sitting in the late night bar,
I fingered a bottle cap while
another tragic love story
streamed through my head.
The light from a beer sign
reflected off the whiskey glass
to form a shimmering horizon
that gently cradled the cap.
That's when I realized
sunrises can happen
whenever and wherever
we need them.

From Afar

Sometimes I think I love best
from afar,
observing impossible conquests
from behind crowds
of maniacs on sidewalks.
Sometimes I love through written notes
to people in faraway places.
When up close, reality stops
the imaginings.
I dream of far better love
than I live.

Scents of Replacement

At night, the fresh sweat
that rolls down succulent breasts,
the vodka, bourbon, and wine
that pours down guilty throats,
and good tobacco smoke
that hovers below the lights,
all of it carries the scent
of animal passions
released into the wild.

In the morning, those same smells
grow old, stale, out of favor.
Betrayal replaces desire
as vomit replaces the splendor of semen.
The reality of regret
that stares back at us in the mirror
through bloodshot eyes
forever replaces another slice
of innocence.

Burn for it

If we truly desire
to seek and find kindness,
we must navigate
the fires of Hell.
Only in torment,
possessions lost, can we give
ourselves to another
without pretense.

Secretions

At 6:00, I drank
to remember,
to swim in the nectar
of consequences secreted
over a lifetime.
At midnight, I drank
to forget.

Dream Down

In my younger years, I dreamt
about flying over lakes and mountains,
and I dreamt about fucking
slutty women in sleazy motels.
Sometimes I battled noble samurai
on ancient Japanese hillsides.

Throughout my life, I've lived out
those subconscious musings
in one form or another.

Now, I rarely remember dreams.
The few that stand out are simple
reflections of life's boring troubles.
Maybe the trick is to find new adventures
that will keep our dreamscapes active,
interesting, forever alive.

Dating Site Interaction #78

Her: Hello.

Me: Why is your name 'SunMoonGoddess'?

Her: It just sounds cool.

Me: I like whiskey.

Her: Are you drunk?

Me: Whatever...as if

Her: Ok then

Me: Date drunk. Edit sober.

Her: What?

Me: Can I have sex with you?

Her: Have fun

Me: Yes?

Her: Do not contact me again.

Thanksgiving

I've never preferred turkey.
That bland taste is the reminder
of the bland jobs and the lovers
with bland imaginations.
When we give thanks,
I bow my head in reverence
for the perpetual fight.
That dash of ferment
snatches a glimmer of life
from the march toward
our insipid decline.

Overcome the Darkness

I lost the job.
The next day,
I lost the woman.
Later came the insomnia,
the denial, the escapes.
A friend said,
'There is no God,'
so I lost that communion
and I lost the friend.

Betrayed by a setting sun,
rain clouds shrouded the stars.
The streetlight on the corner
flickered on and off, on and off.
After a minute, the bulb stopped
its exhaustive dance.

I stepped outside
into the nothingness
in my stocking feet.
Road dirt would blacken the socks.
Not giving a damn about the trivialities
hit the throat like a smoky scotch.

Fools in torment, they know how to find perspective.

Alone in the quiet dark,
not a car in sight,
a gentle feminine voice spoke.
'If you're ready, just say so.'
Startled, my chest tightened.

I squinted to peer through the black.
'Only sleeping robins will know,'
the voice said. 'It's okay.'

I raised my arms,
palms opened, fingers straight.
A chuckle parted my lips.
I didn't even try to stop it.
The laughs then boomed.
Neighborhood dogs barked.
All those perfect church ladies,
they turned out to be right.
Only the damned howl
into the void.

The streetlight then flickered
on and off, on and off.
I walked back inside,
climbed into bed,
and slept.

Shielded

I stood in a pool of piss
in front of the urinal
after watching a beautiful film
about a man who gets the girl.
Irrational tears clouded my vision
and blocked the putrid scents
of real life.
My body wanted me
to live in that story
a little longer.
That was nice.

Better Drunk

Everything is better when drunk
on whiskey and ginger ale.
Paying bills, fucking, music,
even listening to the screams
of former lovers curse you
into damnation.
Fashionable liars prefer beer.
Poets who write in meter
and rhyme, they drink wine.
I am not most poets.

Howl and Chase

I really have no idea
how anyone can love a writer.
We're great observers,
but terrible people.
Marry a carpenter or a welder.
They know how to build
things worthy of your heart.
All a writer can do is howl
at the moon in madness
and chase the dreams
that never come.

Hopping About

When a man gets married,
they say he is shackled or imprisoned.
When a woman doesn't have a man,
they say she isn't living
to her full potential.

Sitting on a sidewalk bench
near the job, two robins landed
in the mulch around a tree.
The birds poked each other a bit
with their beaks and hopped about.
One robin then took off into the limitless sky.
A second later, the other followed.

I never bothered to ask the birds
to define their relationship.
They seemed quite happy
with the way things were.

Sweat

When a drop of sweat
from your chin lands between
a lover's breasts, some women
will recoil in disgust.
Others will moan
and get off on your labor
to deliver great pleasure.

A big lesson we learn over the years
is that the dame who digs a little sweat
during the younger years
will mop it from your forehead
in the nursing home.

On the Lookout

When I had joy,
I didn't know it.
When the joy left,
that's when I knew.
I've been trying
to get the joy back.
That work is a struggle.
There's sweat and strife.
Still, I'm optimistic.
The joy will return.

Drivers and Riders

Love is the act
of moving forward.
When we're young,
we shovel coal into the fire
to build speed.
The older we get,
the flames dwindle.

Some of us hit gyms
and yoga classes
to reclaim the love
that slipped away.
Madmen conquer.
Hustlers get sloppy.
The dames whore.

Others get drunk
on the roofs of slow trains
and remember love
while gazing in awe
at sunsets
we can't control.

Dating Site Interaction #942

Me: Want to go on a date?

Her: I don't date dummies.

Me: I'm only half dumb.

Her: We can go out if you answer a question.

Me: Shoot.

Her: Where are Cornish games hens from?

Me: Cornwall, UK.

Her: No... They come from Cornia.

Me: You either despise me or you hate books.

Her: Sorry.

Stretched Fingers

At times, I feel so alone.
I reach out to people,
yet they do not respond.
Others refuse to make contact.
Funny.
Solitude is a toxic lover.
She promises liberation
and inspires creativity.
Her fangs are hidden
behind those soft, wet lips,
under seductive eyes.
She waits to strike.
Anticipation
is its own reward.

Loving Torture

One morning I awoke
to the sounds of birds
arguing, bickering, disagreeing
about the location of worms
and the meaning of life.
I hollered out the window,
'Shut the fuck up,' but they refused
to respect the order of the food chain.
Streaks of lost love clouded my vision.
Someday, I figured, I'd get back to it—
the words and the women.
As the chirping bored into my brain,
I knew it would not be that day.
My penance is a craven appetite
for never-ending torment.

The Chance

There are opportunities
to make life bearable,
such as winning a buck
on the pool table or getting a wink
from the woman every drunkard
masturbates to in the men's room.
These gifts are sent by angels
that wager on which sap
will miss his chance.

Keep one eye open, baby.
If you're not careful,
you too may become the butt
of the next cosmic joke.

Creep Forward

At a North Side red light,
I watched her cross the street,
my hands glued to the steering wheel.
The rest of the city went dim.
All I could see was her little dress,
bare legs that glimmered, heels,
hips like handles -- they begged
for a purpose, a reason.
The muted sound of car horns blared
in some distant background.
A man's voice screamed.

Once the dame stepped onto the curb,
her little dress twirled
and she shot me the finger,
a just punishment for the rape.
A deep breath,
a stroke of the beard,
the car crept forward.
'Thanks, baby,' I whispered.
That was the best sex I'd had
in quite some time.

Convenient Love

A dead Christmas tree
was set out with a neighbor's trash.
It lay sideways, stripped
of half its needles.
A brown cat sniffed
one of its branches,
but then sauntered away.
All relationships eventually
lose their charm.

Pleasant Frame

A good book of verse,
that chair next to the lamp,
a bottle of whiskey
still heavy with escape,
and a good memory
of her. Holy shit.
Maybe it is possible
to thrive.

Repetitive Rhymes

When a woman spreads her thighs,
that's her silent promise
to deliver satisfaction.
When a man professes adoration,
that's his vocal promise
to deliver love.
Lies or truths,
we tend to repeat
these rhyming exploits
all our lives.
Eventually, the day comes
when the body sags
and the mind grows tired
of that same old song.

That One Defender

I've been thinking about you
here and there during recent days.
I wonder if you're doing well
or if life has continued to wear
away at your beauty,
that inner strength I adore.
You are my friend,
yet we live very different lives
in very different worlds.
Regardless of the differences,
you mean the world to me.
No matter where we live
or who we love and loathe,
I am forever comforted
that you are my friend
until the end.

Dating Site Interaction #487

Me: Hey there. Do you like grilled cheese?

Her: Grilled cheese is a must!

Me: Awesome. What's your name?

Her: What's yours?

Me: Ron

Her: Okay Ronald

Me: Ron. What's your name?

Her: I don't give out my contact info

Me: You know this is a dating site, right?

Her: So?

Me: Okay.

Bad Butt

You and I had parallel routines
at the same time of the day,
yet we never really met.
Nevertheless, I loved you
from across rooms
and across streets.
The way you laughed
gave me reason to write
and walk in the sun.
Then the day came
when I saw you shove
your entire hand down your pants
to pick out a butt wedgie.
That's when I knew
the love was gone.

Dating Site Interaction #523

Me: You're really attractive.

Her: Thanks I guess.

Me: Are you a reader?

Her: I don't know.

Me: It's okay if you don't read, as long as you're a screamer.

Her: That was inappropriate.

Me: You're right!

Her: Relationships are about compromise.

Me: Yes! Compromise. You have to split the difference.

Her: Right.

Me: So, let's compromise. I want to have sex with you 96 times. You want to have sex with me 0 times. Now, what's the compromise?

Her: How about I don't kick you in the balls?

Me: Hey! You changed the parameters of the compromise.

Her: Can you go away now?

Me: Sure.

Imperfect Laughs

Beautiful women
never really dug me.
The really sexy ones
of wealth and privilege,
they have their asses kissed
regularly by lady's men
in designer suits.
I've never been good
at projecting sweet lies
onto diseased souls.
So, I seek damaged women
acquainted with pain,
that bitter hit of disappointment.
Those dames can smell
bullshit from across streets.
They understand hardship,
pursue truth, and laugh
like the end is near.

Elusive Love

The most romantic moment
I've ever lived happened in a city park
during a human rights rally.
A sexy brunette made eyes at me
and my tattoos. I waved to her.
She grinned and waved back.
Later on, while a speaker shared
his thoughts on aiding the poor,
that same woman raised her fist
and proclaimed we are all
brothers and sisters.
Afterwards, she was gone.
She had vanished
in the crowd.

Designed to Suffer

The women of dignity
we love unconditionally
up close and from afar,
they are designed to suffer.
The torment of false lovers
and failed promises
flickers right behind their eyes.
Small expressions of love from we
who live in silent desperation,
that's the fuel our women use
to fend off the demons
and care for us
all their lives.

A title here would only admit defeat

Alone
is sneezing
while chewing
on your dinner
and thinking
you might choke
Loneliness
is then whispering
'Bless you'
to yourself

Good Memories

Good memories
drip slowly through the mind
They are drops of spring rain
that fall on my shoulders
from the train bridge
above the sidewalk
where we talked
for hours.

Worth the Time

Don't worry so much.
Short love is easy,
but it's the long game
that eludes most lonely souls.
Men and women through history
have lived entire lives
falling in and out
of that gravitational pull.
You and I may never get there.
That's okay.
The pursuit over gritty foothills,
the pitfalls, and the consequences
are what keeps it interesting.
The dream makes our 80 years
well worth the time.

A little poorer
in the wallet
and a little richer
in spirit,
all of us finish
alone.

About the Author

Ron Gavalik is a writer
in Pittsburgh, Pennsylvania.
You can stalk him online.
He likes whiskey.

Made in the USA
Middletown, DE
28 February 2023

25825898R00089